Circle Time

A Lucky Duck Book

Circle Time

A Resource Book for Primary and Secondary Schools

Second Edition

Teresa Bliss and Jo Tetley

P·C·P
Paul Chapman
Publishing

Paul Chapman Publishing
P·C·P   A SAGE Publications Company
Paul Chapman
Publishing
1 Oliver's Yard
55 City Road UNIVERSITY OF CHICHESTER
London EC1Y 1SP

SAGE Publications Inc.
2455 Teller Road
Thousand Oaks, California 91320

SAGE Publications India Pvt Ltd.
B-42, Panchsheel Enclave
Post Box 4109
New Delhi 110 017

www.luckyduck.co.uk

Commissioning Editor: George Robinson
Editorial Team: Mel Maines, Sarah Lynch, Wendy Ogden
Designer: Jess Wright

A catalogue record for this book is available from the British Library
Library of Congress Control Number 2006920673

ISBN13 978-1-4129-2026-1
ISBN10 1-4129-2026-4

Printed on paper from sustainable resources
Printed in Great Britain by The Cromwell Press Ltd, Trowbridge, Wiltshire

Contents

Acknowledgements

With thanks to our colleagues in Gloucestershire County Council, Elton Project 1990 – 1993.

In memory

Circle Time is used widely in schools because teachers and young people love it. Nobody told us to do it – the word spread and amongst those who carried the word was a remarkable bookseller called Madeleine Lindley. She promoted Circle Time with enthusiasm – teachers responded by finding a place in the curriculum for Circle Time. Thank you.

Preface

We started using Circle Time in Primary Schools in 1990 as part of the social education programme because we knew that properly used it can lead to the enhancing of pupils' self-esteem and improved relationships and behaviour within the classroom. We had positive feedback from pupils and staff who saw it as an enjoyable and worthwhile experience with many unexpected bonuses. Our first book was written because at that time there were very few texts suitable for Circle Time and with the exception of Murray White's work no one in this country was specifically writing on Circle Time for teachers. Mosley's first book (1996) followed shortly after the publication of our first edition with Bromfield and Curry's *Personal and Social Education for Primary Schools Through Circle Time* being published in the following year. Taylor (2003) has reviewed current research and practice in Circle Time. She inevitably calls for more research however, the findings she quotes in her case-studies frequently reflects our experience in our work.

In his foreword to that first edition of *Circle Time* written in 1993, George Robinson wrote that:

> Whilst Circle Time has an obvious part to play in the curriculum as an opportunity to develop speaking and listening, it should be seen as fulfilling an essential role in the Spiritual and Moral development of young people.

He then talked about the way Circle Time could be used to support the implementation of aspects of the Spiritual and Moral Curriculum most notably the following elements:

- self-knowledge
- relationships
- feelings and emotions.

Goleman (1995) emphasised the key role of emotional intelligence in our lives. His work has led to the expansion of the thinking evident in the earlier documents from the government. More recently the DFES 2004 document *Every Child Matters: Change for Children in Schools* sets guidelines on how schools can improve the outcomes for children and young people with its emphasis on the fact that pupil performance and emotional wellbeing go hand in hand. In the document *Every Child Matters* the five national outcomes for children and young people are described as:

- being healthy
- staying safe
- enjoying and achieving

- making a positive contribution

- economic wellbeing.

The values and attitudes which Circle Time was aimed at enhancing are now seen as central to creating a 'healthy school'. To become a 'healthy school' schools need to provide evidence that the standards are being met in these key areas. The National Children's Bureau's belief about best practice in *Personal, Social and Health Education* (1993) states that:

> Children and young people need support in developing emotionally and socially so that they are able to use their thoughts and feelings to guide their behaviour positively and develop personal awareness, emotional resilience and social skills... A healthy school is one that works to develop a whole school ethos, environment and curriculum that enables pupils to recognise personal qualities, build on achievements, do their best and manage their health and wellbeing.

The continuing influence of Goleman's (op cit) work is evident in the next element of the government's primary strategies published in June 2005, *Social and Emotional Aspects of Learning.* Circle Time is used as a vehicle to promote many of the activities to develop core elements:

- self-awareness

- empathy

- managing feelings

- self-motivation

- social skills.

We know that Circle Time can play a vital part in achieving these aims especially when used throughout the school on a regular basis as part of the weekly timetable. Certainly we know it helps children think about their own behaviour and responses to situations.

> Public acknowledgement and peer encouragement in the circle can be powerful motivators for change... (teachers) derive satisfaction from children's enjoyment and gain new insights into their pupils... Moreover, a common involvement of teachers in Circle Time may make for greater staff interaction at all levels in sharing teaching and learning experiences and support.

(Taylor 2003, p148-9)

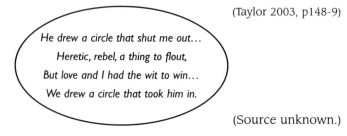

He drew a circle that shut me out...
Heretic, rebel, a thing to flout,
But love and I had the wit to win...
We drew a circle that took him in.

(Source unknown.)

x

Introduction

Circle Time brings together teacher and children in an enjoyable atmosphere of cooperation. It is a time set aside each week when children and their teacher sit in a circle and take part in games and activities designed to increase self-awareness, awareness of others, self-esteem, cooperation, trust and listening skills. The activity helps everyone to understand what is important to them and their friends. Children become more able to express their feelings and it encourages greater tolerance between girls and boys. As children learn more about themselves and each other a warm and supportive group atmosphere is built, along with improved relationships.

Self-esteem

For teachers the issue of a child's self-esteem is a vitally important consideration. Self-esteem affects a child's behaviour in all aspects of school life including academic and social. Research has shown strong links between positive self-esteem and success at school. Children with a positive high self-regard are more likely to achieve academically and are less likely to be in trouble than children with low self-regard.

Below are listed some of the behaviour traits that might indicate low self-regard:

- feeling uncomfortable with praise
- unable to accept praise
- unable to ask for needs to be met
- critical and jealous of others
- inability to be warm and affectionate
- being negative about self and particularly in comparison with others
- feeling unworthy and guilty
- refusing to work in case of failure.

The games in Circle Time aim to break into those feelings, in a gentle and subtle way they encourage everyone to:

- praise themselves (I'm good at…)
- talk positively about self and achievements
- be assertive about needs

- give and accept compliments in a matter of fact way
- accept that things go wrong sometimes yet it need not fundamentally impinge on self-worth
- celebrate achievements and good times
- be prepared to take risks, to have a go at unfamiliar work or activities.

National Curriculum

Circle Time meets the demands of the National Curriculum in many areas, for example, English and Spiritual and Moral development. It is also a tool of the Primary Strategy for Social and Emotional Aspects of Learning (SEAL). Circle Time requires children to participate as speakers and listeners in whole-class activities and to respond appropriately to simple and complex instructions given by both teacher and pupils and to accurately convey simple messages.

Listening and speaking

When we introduced Circle Time to schools teachers were exceptionally pleased with the impact it had on listening and speaking skills. Listening, in particular, is mentioned time and again. It also helps children to be patient and wait their turn. In the circle all children eventually have the opportunity to speak. They become better at waiting as they become more tolerant of others. The teacher is able to model acceptance and be non-judgmental.

Rules for the circle

We believe rules should be kept to a minimum, for example, no more than one or two at a session. We usually only introduce the first rule; sometimes the first and the second rules are all that is required. However, we suggest you allow the rules to evolve as necessary. Sometimes the same rule needs to be introduced time and again in different contexts with some classes and for particular individuals, but this is, after all, how we teach anything. Below is a list of rules we have needed from time to time, but we want to emphasise they may not all be needed.

- We listen when someone else is speaking.
- We may pass.
- We don't remind anyone else what he/she should be doing.
- There are no 'put downs.'

You will find some children like to test the pass rule for one or two rounds. The novelty soon wears off.

Sometimes children are silly, for example, a child may say, 'I like to beat up my sister'. It is best to ignore such a statement and move on in as neutral a way as possible. On the other hand it may be more appropriate to say dispassionately, 'I haven't given you much time to think, I'll come back to you'. This gives the child the opportunity to redeem himself with a more acceptable statement. It is also a sharing of the responsibility. It is important to remember that everyone is equal within the circle and the interactions are not child to teacher but child to the circle.

Circle ethos and benefits

The ethos of Circle Time is positive, encouraging and non-judgemental.

Children thoroughly enjoy Circle Time. They appreciate the opportunity to be listened to and to know that their turn will come. They enjoy hearing personal details about their teacher. They love being encouraged to feel that they are important and likeable individually and collectively.

The children one would least expect often plan and think through what their contribution will be. The articulation of their views and ideas improves along with the listening skills we have already mentioned. The circle can become a forum where class members are able to express their needs, negotiate and mediate. All this reduces the likelihood of problems and frustrations. Towards the end of the book there are suggestions on how Circle Time can help with friendship problems and open up the topic of bullying. Our experience tells us that teachers use it in creative and imaginative ways that are best for their unique situations.

Benefits for teachers

Taylor (2003) helped to clarify our thinking on this aspect of Circle Time. She found:

- Teachers learned through doing Circle Time and became aware of their own pedagogical needs.

- Circle Time could act as a control on young children's discipline. (Also that indiscipline could undermine Circle Time.)

- Teachers learned to be aware of children's feelings and to listen to them...they came to know their pupils as individuals more quickly and raised their expectations.

- Circle Time helped quiet and reluctant children to communicate.

- Overall, teachers thought children improved their self-esteem and confidence, respect and support for their peers and developed communication skills from Circle Time.

Taylor also found that teachers benefited from being trained in Circle Time and that members of the leadership team were often better trained than other members of staff. Furthermore, very occasionally there were members of staff who found it very difficult to do Circle Time. While an issue such as this is for individual managers to resolve we recommend that these teachers are supported and that it may be better for another member of staff who is more comfortable with the activities to take Circle Time.

Overall, Taylor's findings reflect our experience in that Circle Time not only benefits children but teachers as well. It is valuable for all those involved.

Organisation of Circle Time

It is best done in the classroom where you can keep the warm atmosphere you generate. The beginning or end of a session is the easiest time to rearrange chairs and desks. We would recommend that chairs are placed in a circle, leaving the centre free for movement within the circle. If the children are seated on the floor, as they get up and move around, the circle becomes distorted and the space they need to return to is lost. Opportunities for listening and eye contact between all participants is a priority. We have found that the session runs much more smoothly if children are comfortable.

The activities should last for about twenty minutes to half an hour. Most children appreciate a familiar ending activity.

The games

We have decided to retain the word 'games' even though it can be interchangeable with the word 'activities' because *Every Child Matters* (DFES 2004) suggests that children learn through fun and Circle Time, as teachers who have been using it for many years know, is a good example of that. The games in this book are used to have fun and to deal with serious issues.

Most of the games listed are suitable for all ages. So many times infant teachers have commented to us how surprised they were by the level of articulation and understanding. Colleagues will know which games are suitable for their classes. Many of them are adaptable, for example, the game Finishing the Sentence we use with infant and adult groups and all ages in between. Many of the games have variations on the theme, and we have listed the ones we know. We have called the Circle Time leader the facilitator because eventually it may be possible for the children to lead the sessions rather than the teacher.

Paired work and small groups

Working in small groups is a natural progression in Circle Time and it enables children to explore and discuss more challenging and serious topics in a non-threatening way, i.e. dealing with conflict, family relationships and self-harm.

Sources

Most of the games in this book are adaptations and variations devised by us over the years to suit the needs of the children and schools we have worked with.

Over the years we have used a great many sources. Some games have passed into common usage, others were given to us with the origin unknown. Many games are familiar to those in the Brownie and Guide and Cub and Scout movements. Books that either we have found useful or have been recommended to us are listed in the reference section.

Summarisation

Circle Time encourages:

- cognitive skills such as the ability to reflect, predict, question, concentrate, evaluate then recount in a concise manner

- interpersonal skills such as the ability to listen, explain feelings and motives, empathise, encourage others in a positive way and speak publicly

- a compassionate, sensitive and accepting attitude to others, developed in a spirit of generosity, openness and caring.

To do this:

- Positive, simple rules are followed.
- Feelings are focused on.
- Awareness of self and others is encouraged.
- No judgements are made (by teachers or children).
- Personal responsibility is emphasised.
- Each member is valued.
- Everyone experiences sharing in a sensitive, positive yet fun way.

Developmental Aspects of Circle Time through Key Stages 1 to 3

Circle Time is developmental. The developmental progression can be identified at the first three key stages. Although regardless of age, if Circle Time is being introduced for the first time then the teacher needs to ensure that students have the Key Stage 1 skills in order to participate fully and successfully.

Key Stage 1

Key Stage 1 should focus on:

- acquiring a vocabulary:
    - how to pronounce words
    - understanding the meaning of those words
    - have a vocabulary of affirmation and feelings words that is likely to be specific to Circle Time
- controlling impulsive or unrestrained behaviours such as calling out
- learning to take turns and wait patiently
- learning to focus and concentrate
- learning to listen within the circle
- learning to remember what has been said
- learning to respond appropriately in a positive and affirming way
- becoming aware of self as an individual as well as self as a member of a group; recognising uniqueness and commonalities.

Key Stage 1: Example Lesson

Introduction: Remind the children about the rules before they need to use them.

1. A Starting Game: My Name (p16)

   (The facilitator starts, going around the circle from their left.)

   My name is... and so on around the circle.

2. Silent Statements – to change places (p26)

   Stand up and change places all children wearing something blue, laces on their shoes, grey socks, wearing a cardigan, etc.

3. Finishing the Sentence (p38)

   (The facilitator starts going around the circle from their right.)

   My favourite colour is...

   (Go back to the child who couldn't say a colour, to encourage them to have a turn.)

4. A Finishing Game: Pass the Smile (p56)

   (The facilitator starts, going round circle from their left.)

   Make eye contact with person to your left and smile and so on around the circle.

Key Stage 2

As children continue to work with Circle Time through this Key Stage they reinforce and build upon learning at Key Stage 1. The focus of Key Stage 2 teaching and learning will be:

- developing a vocabulary that is understood and used appropriately in context

- taking turns with ease and grace

- remembering what is said

- beginning to feed back information as a critical friend who is able to be positive and affirming

- being able to verbalise own beliefs, opinions and thoughts

- understanding the difference between assertive and aggressive dialogue

- being able to engage assertively in dialogue with peers with opposing views

- understanding one's own strengths and weaknesses within the context of the group

- for the group to understand and accept others' strengths and weaknesses

- learning to give and receive affirmations

- to develop empathy

- becoming aware of the negative effects of antisocial behaviour and the benefits of pro-social behaviour.

Key Stage 2: Example Lesson

Introduction: Remind the pupils about the rules before they need to use them.

1. A Starting Game: My Name – and the name of the person on my right (p16)

2. Silent Statements (p26)

   Stand up and change places all those:

   - who are wearing buckles on their shoes

   - wearing a 'V' neck jumper

   - who can swim a width of the pool

   - who enjoy using the computer

   - who watch (favourite 'soap') on TV.

3. Finishing the Sentence (p38)

   My favourite animal is... because...

4. 50 Ways of Moving (p46)

5. Finishing the Sentence (p38)

   The thing I like doing best in school is...

6. A Finishing Game: Pass the Squeeze (p56)

Key Stage 3

While Circle Time is a valuable tool and can be introduced to this Key Stage there can be some difficulties for young people, as they move into their teenage years they often become more self-conscious and less willing to make a mistake in public that may lead to embarrassment and humiliation. It is essential therefore that the work for Circle Time is appropriate for the ability level as well as the age group. Particular care needs to be taken with the use of language.

Children at Key Stage 3 may be used to working with Circle Time. They may understand the process and have developed the key stage skills mentioned earlier. If that is the case then young people are likely to come into this key stage with:

- good listening skills
- an understanding of an assertive response
- some understanding of body language
- a good vocabulary to express feelings
- a proficiency of retaining the Circle Time process and working with it
- a sense of selves
- an ability to express their own opinions.

It is increasingly likely that children leaving Key Stage 2 who have had Circle Time and followed the SEAL programme will have developed their emotional intelligence and be well versed with emotionally literate skills.

Particular areas that often need a teaching and learning developmental focus include:

- understanding how to be empathic and to respond accordingly
- continuing to increase the affective vocabulary
- initiating and leading problem solving activities in the social arena
- being critical friends to themselves and others and being able to accept such help
- accurately predicting and judging social situations and responding appropriately
- becoming comfortable and genuine in affirming others
- accepting affirmations with ease and good grace.

Key Stage 3: Example Lesson

Introduction: Remind students about the rules before they need to use them.

1. A Starting Game: My Name – introduce self and person to left or right (p16)

2. Silent Statements (p26)

Stand up and change places all those who:

   • have been to the cinema recently

   • watched a favourite 'soap' this week

   • enjoy eating chocolate.

3. Finishing the Sentence (p38)

   • When I am older I would like to be… because…

   • I think all parents should…

   • One thing that would make school better is if we…

4. Partners (p36)

Find something that we both enjoy doing.

5. A Finishing Game: Guess Who – Game 2 (p43)

Part I

The Games

Introducing Games

These games help children use their own names and names of classmates. They encourage a positive group feeling and help develop self-esteem and awareness of peers.

My Name and Variations

Aim: Encourages the development of the ability to say one's own name confidently and publicly, taking turns and self-awareness.

Game 1

For the very young ones (three to five years) the facilitator starts by saying, 'My name is…' and then encourages each child in the circle to say their name in turn around the circle using the whole sentence.

Game 2

The facilitator starts by saying, 'My name is Miss Jones.' The first student to her right says, 'My name is John and this is Miss Jones.' This process is continued around the circle until each person has said their name and introduced the person on their left.

Game 3

Say your name and introduce the people sitting either side.

Game 4

Each person introduces themselves and says how they feel: 'My name is Miss Jones and I'm feeling tired.'

Game 5

Introduce yourself with an adjective that begins with the same letter as your name, e.g. 'I am careful Colin.'

Game 6

Introduce yourself with a verb, e.g. 'I am Henry, hopping Henry'.

Helpful hint

- Talking about and making lists of 'feeling words', adjectives and verbs (for Games 4, 5 and 6) is a good idea before the game starts.

Up Down Up

Aim: Encourages the development of cooperation and working sequentially.

This game looks very impressive watched from outside the circle.

Game 1

Everyone sits in a circle; when they say their name they stand up then sit down immediately. Each person in the circle will stand up once.

Game 2

The facilitator starts the game by saying the name of the person to their right, their own name, then the name of the person to the left and each time a name is called the person stands up then sits down immediately.

Each person in the circle will stand up three times.

Helpful hint

- Game 1 first.

Ball Rolling

Aim: Encourages the development of how to affirm another person and how to accept a compliment.

Game 1

First person calls out the name of the person they have chosen and rolls the ball to them. That person then calls out the name of someone else and rolls the ball, and so on until everyone has had a turn.

Game 2

A child calls the name of the person she intends to roll the ball to and says something they like to do, e.g. 'Emma, I like skipping', and rolls the ball to Emma.

Materials

Soft ball.

Helpful hint

- Remind them to listen and remember who has had a turn so that each person's name is only called once.

Web Masters

Aim: Encourages the development of how to affirm another person and how to accept a compliment.

Game 1

The ball of wool is gradually unravelled as it is passed across and around the circle. The first person unravels a length of string, holds the end of the string, then throws the ball across to someone saying 'I am throwing this to...' At the end of all the string look at the connections that have been made.

Game 2

The same process is followed. The young people say, 'I am throwing this to... because she/he is... (put in a positive social attribute e.g. fun).

Game 3

Again the same process. 'I am throwing this to... because she/he is... (put in positive attribute related to working/helping in class).

Materials

Large ball of string or wool.

Helpful hint

- If using wool make sure you have a strong enough ply to withstand the strain of young people pulling on it.

Name Association

Aim: Encourages the development of self-awareness and managing feelings.

A child is asked to talk about his name, for example:

I like my name because...

I don't like my name because...

I would like my name to have been...

Other people with my name in my family are...

My parents chose my name because...

An adjective that goes well with my name...

An adjective that reflects my name...

Helpful hints

- This game runs better if the facilitator starts the game with a clear example so that the children know what sort of response to make.

- It is more suitable for Key Stages 2 and 3.

Name Chain

Aim: Encourages the development of cooperation, listening and remembering who has had a turn.

Each person moves once to the chair of the named person, i.e. Jo calls Mary and moves to Mary's chair, Mary calls Peter and moves to Peter's chair...

Helpful hint

- Remind children to give everyone a turn.

Action Mime

Aim: Encourages the development of concentration and observation.

The first person does one action, e.g. clap hands. The second person copies that mime and does one of their own, e.g. claps hands and clicks fingers. The third person copies the last action and adds one of their own, e.g. clicks fingers and smiles. Continue around the circle, each child doing two actions each.

Helpful hint

- The facilitator needs to demonstrate this first with the two people next to her and maybe have half a circle practice round.

All Change Games

These games are sometimes known as 'energisers'. They allow teachers to move friendship groups or troublesome groups in a subtle and fun way, also the group can be changed during the session so children can work with new partners. It may be necessary if children are excitable, to remind them about moving across the circle quietly without touching anyone.

Postman

Aim: Encourages the development of listening, memory, cooperation and sequential thinking.

Game 1

The facilitator gives everyone a number.

The facilitator calls out, 'The postman is calling at numbers two and twelve'.

Children with these numbers change places.

If the call is 'collection time' all change places.

Game 2

Remove one chair from the circle. A child stands in the centre of the circle.

The facilitator calls out, 'The postman is coming to… (two numbers). The child in the centre tries to reach a chair whilst the changeover takes place. (Only two goes in the centre are allowed.)

Game 3

The postman is going to all the odd numbers. The postman is going to the even numbers. Collection time.

Helpful hints

- Remind the children to listen carefully when you give them a number. It helps them to remember if you touch the child on each shoulder and have eye contact, and when you have given each child a number check that they have remembered it.

- You may need to explain how we traditionally numbered our houses. New housing estates are often numbered differently.

- This game can be adapted for a maths session to teach odd and even numbers.

Follow Me

Aim: Encourages the development of listening and following directions.

Game 1

The facilitator gives simple directions, for example:

- take a step forward
- touch toes
- hands on head
- the class to follow directions.

Game 2

Simon says, giving quicker instructions.

Helpful hint

- Remind children to keep watching and listening and proceed slowly until they become familiar with the process.

Trains, Boats and Planes

Aim: Encourages the development of memory, listening, following instructions, cooperation and taking turns.

Game 1

Sit in a circle.

Each child is touched and told whether he is a train, boat or plane.

If the facilitator calls out 'boats' the boats change places. If she calls out 'transport' they all change places.

The facilitator removes one chair so that someone is left in the middle. They call out what is to move. Everyone should have one turn in the middle.

Game 2

Children are named crocodiles, elephants and giraffes. Each animal is mimed, for example, crocodiles extend arms and clap hands to show snapping mouths.

The facilitator calls out who is to move and the children change places (most suitable for children aged three to five).

Helpful hints

- When telling each child what they are going to be, make eye contact and put your hand on each shoulder – it helps them to remember.

- This is a good opportunity for the shy child to have the chance to instruct others. If it is played for too long the dominant ones hang back to be the last to sit down.

My Eyes Are...

Aim: Encourages the development of self-awareness.

Game 1

The facilitator and the children sit in a circle.

The facilitator calls out an eye colour.

All those with eyes that colour change seats.

Game 2

This game can be used as a way of pairing children, for example, the facilitator says all those with brown eyes stand up and come to the middle, now find a friend from the centre to sit next to.

Helpful hint

- More suitable for Key Stage 2 and older children because Key Stage 1 children are unlikely to know their own eye colour.

The Sun Will Come Out...

Aim: Encourages the development of affirmation, an effective vocabulary and cooperation.

Game 1

The facilitator and the children sit in a circle.

The facilitator says, 'The sun will come out for children who...' The facilitator then chooses a suitable sentence stub, for example:

- are happy
- have been kind to someone
- have helped their parents today
- have helped a friend today.

Children who relate to this stand up and change places.

Game 2

The same game script is used as in Game 1 but the circle has one chair short and the facilitator (child or facilitator) stands in the middle to say the script and as people in the circle change places the facilitator tries to get to a chair leaving a new person in the middle.

Helpful hints

- If the children are already familiar with other 'All Change' games such as Trains, Boats and Planes it will make introducing these games easier.
- The Sun Will Come Out... is best played with Key Stage 2 and Key Stage 3 children.
- Game 1 needs to be familiar before playing Game 2.

New Friends

Aim: Encourages the development of cooperation.

Place chairs in a circle. The children and the facilitator fill the floor space inside the circle.

All walk slowly round looking down. They are told not to look at or bump into anyone else.

Each person is touched on the shoulder by the facilitator and asked their name. They then sit down quietly.

Helpful hint

- This is a good game for the beginning of term. It is also a game you can use with a new child being the facilitator.

Silent Statements

Aim: Encourages the development of self-awareness and self-regulation, motivation, managing feelings and developing empathy.

We use this game every time; it is a way of making a statement about ourselves without speaking. Silent Statements can be adapted for any theme. It has many names – one of our favourites is 'The Washing Line'.

Children need to be told that if the statement applies to them then they need to stand up and change places with someone else also standing.

The facilitator makes a statement, for example:

all children wearing… (colours, certain clothes, etc.)

all children who can… (ride a bike, swim a width, etc.)

all children with… (missing teeth, a brother, blue eyes, etc.)

all children who watch… (Neighbours, The Bill, etc.)

all children who will be… (ten next birthday, going on holiday, etc.)

More Silent Statements suggested are: 'Change places if…'

you enjoy eating pizza, roast beef, cornflakes

you enjoy reading

you hate having a bath

you love watching football

you watch TV before school in the mornings

your birthday is this term

you have never stayed away from home

you are concerned about the environment

friends are very important to you

you have a pet at home

your eyes are blue/brown

you agree with school uniform

you would like to wear different clothes to school

to get to school you walk, cycle come by bus, car, train.

Helpful hints

- For very young children (three to five years) this can be broken down very simply. For example, ask the children to look, very quietly, at the clothes they are wearing today: 'Look at our shoes and the colour they are and if they have laces or buckles. Then look at our socks, etc. and so on until we touch our hair, to see if we are wearing a ribbon or a hair band. Then put our hands on our laps.'

  The instructions could be:

  'Let's look at our shoes again'.

  'If you have laces on your shoes please stand up'.

  'Go to the middle of the circle'.

  'Now find a different seat to sit in'.

- Ensure you give the full sentence and the instruction to stand up and change places each time.

- See *Developing Circle Time* (1995).

Games to Encourage Self-awareness

These help all children feel really good about themselves and because classmates have contributed to each individual's good feeling, the whole class group has a positive, caring atmosphere.

Statement Line

Aim: Encourages the development of self-awareness, awareness of others, managing feelings, assertiveness and the ability to express feelings and opinions.

This is a useful technique to elicit views without anyone actually saying anything. A good demonstration of how to use it is in Part 2 under the activities for the Bullying theme.

As with all the activities in this book we recommend you have fun with this and become familiar with the process before it is used for a serious purpose.

Game 1

The facilitator indicates an imaginary line across the circle or in another part of the room. The 'line' is a continuum with 'agree' at one end and 'disagree' at the other. The facilitator explains this while walking along the 'line' to establish clearly where it is. The facilitator then makes a statement that the children can choose to agree or disagree with. It is possible to take a range of issues from just fun to very serious to explore using the Statement Line. For example:

'Chocolate is my favourite type of sweet.'

'I think all children should choose their own bedtimes.'

'My least favourite food is pizza.'

'School uniform should be abolished.'

'My favourite activity is tidying up, especially my bedroom.'

Game 2

As in Game 1 an imaginary line is marked out. Then two statements are made followed by a paired discussion and a sentence completion. For example:

'Our prime minister should do all he can to stop child poverty.'

'Personally I would definitely be prepared to donate the cost of a packet of crisps twice a week to a children's charity.'

Discussion

Ask the students to decide how they personally could help 'make poverty history' for children in the developing world.

Plenary

Use the sentence completion:

'Realistically we could...'

Helpful hints

- The line can be contained by removing two chairs opposite each other in the circle.

- Be careful about the concepts at each key stage. Key Stage 1 children can play this game. Keep it to fun decisions and statements at an appropriate developmental level.

I Am Special

Aim: Encourages the development of affirmation, empathy, understanding others, managing feelings and motivation.

The facilitator arranges everyone in a circle, he/she tapes a piece of paper onto each child's back.

The children walk round the circle and write one positive comment on each sheet of paper with a felt tip pen.

When all the comments have been written the children sit back in a circle and read what has been written.

The children take turns to read out one statement that pleases them most.

Materials

A piece of A4 paper for each child, felt tip pens and masking tape.

Helpful hints

- This game is best played with children in Key Stage 2 and Key Stage 3.

- It is important that children understand how to affirm others. At first you may want to have a rule, 'We only ever write positive, nice or good comments.'

It's My Day

Aim: Encourages the development of empathy, the ability to affirm and motivate others.

Game 1

The facilitator chooses one person to go out of the room.

Each child takes turns to say something positive about that person:

'I like... because...'

The facilitator writes the name of the person who has gone out of the room on the paper and all the positive comments made by peers.

The child is called back in and each child reads out the statement he/she has made about the classmate. Or the facilitator reads out the statement, while the child listens.

The written sheet can be taken home.

This is a wonderful game for all ages.

Game 2

Each child has the opportunity to be 'special' once a term. On their special day they could wear a badge and have extra privileges and special jobs to do that they would find rewarding.

Materials

One large sheet of paper and felt tip pens or marker pens.

Helpful hint

- To be seen to be fair, in September you may want to put all children's names on a piece of paper and pull them out of a hat. Then allocate a time during the school year when it will be their turn. All children will see that there is no favouritism and the process for the chosen person will be transparent for all.

This Is Me

Aim: Encourages the development of self-assessment, managing feelings and the ability to make a positive statement about oneself.

The children hold the object, look at their neighbour, turn in their chair and make a positive statement about themselves, for example:

'I like…'

'I am good at…'

'My favourite…'

Materials

An object that is nice to hold.

Helpful hints

- This is a game to encourage making and maintaining appropriate eye contact with a friend.
- This is a very good game for infants or children with poor social skills.
- It is also a good game to use before you ask children to make statements about other children.

Bin It

Aim: Encourages the development of reflecting on unnecessary concerns and managing feelings.

Children often worry unnecessarily about things that adults would not consider important. This game can be quite therapeutic for some children.

Game 1

Before Circle Time the facilitator asks the children to write down one thing in the past that they have worried about unnecessarily and bring it to the circle. The children can have the choice of whether they read out the worry or not. The waste paper bin is placed in the middle of the room and each child in turn puts their unnecessary worry in the bin.

Game 2

Have a sentence completion about unnecessary worries:

'One thing that I worry about unnecessarily in school is… and I am going to try to stop.'

Game 3

Before Circle Time the facilitator asks the children to write down one thing that they are currently worried about but can do nothing about and bring it to the circle. The children can have the choice of whether they read out the worry or not. The waste paper bin is placed in the middle of the room and each child in turn puts their unnecessary worry in the bin while saying that this is one worry they can forget.

Helpful hints

- Keep the worries to school issues. The facilitator might like to model worries to help pupils clarify types of appropriate worries.

- It may be necessary to check with individuals what the worry is before it is declared in the circle.

- These games are more suitable for Key Stage 2 and Key Stage 3 pupils.

Games to Encourage Awareness of Others

These games enable children to express feelings that foster empathy, a better understanding of one another, greater cooperation and trust.

Partners

Aim: Encourages the development of group identity and helps children to think of themselves as members of a group. It also encourages group synergy, communication, emotional awareness, developing sense of self, managing feelings, cooperation and empathy.

Game 1

We suggest children are paired with someone they don't usually work or play with, or play a mixing up game first, for example, the group can be paired off by numbers, fruits, letters or another fun way, i.e. elephant, mouse, elephant, mouse.

The children then turn their chairs to slightly face one another. They share with a partner one or two things they enjoy doing, for example, two television programmes they enjoy. When they are ready, they turn to face the circle, hands on laps. Each child reports back what his partner enjoyed beginning with the sentence stub:

'We liked...' or 'We enjoyed...'

Game 2

The children can share two things they dislike doing or two foods they dislike eating. When children report back ask them to say,

'We dislike...' or 'We don't enjoy...'

Game 3

Divide the group into pairs. Person A tells the other as much as possible about himself, B listens carefully without speaking. After two minutes stop them. Person B then tells about himself while 'A' listens. After four minutes the pairs face the circle. Ask each person to introduce his partner, stating his name and something he has said about himself.

Helpful hints

- This game is useful if you have established cliques and want to broaden friendship groups or wish to help a new child integrate. Some children will need to be supported with the concept 'we'.

- When children report back ask them to say, 'We like...' or 'We enjoy...' You will find that children in Key Stage 1 find the notion of 'we' very difficult. You will most likely have to move round the circle explaining what the word 'we' means. As children grow older we find that the concept 'we' is less difficult to understand.

- Some pairs have to wait a while for their turn and find it hard to resist checking with their partners. Remind them it is important to listen to others and you will allow them to confer again when it is their turn if they need to.

A Brick in the Wall

Aim: Encourages group development and affirmation of others.

Before the circle all the children write, on a Post-it, an affirmation about someone in the class. They bring their own Post-it to the circle.

During Circle Time they read out the person's name and put the Post-it on a prepared sheet to build up an affirmation wall.

Helpful hints

- This will need some preparation before Circle Time for the facilitator to write each child's name on a piece of paper.

- The facilitator should give each child another's name. This ensures that no one is left out.

- Check what the affirmations say before Circle Time begins.

How are they Feeling?

Aim: Encourages the ability to assess others' feelings by facial expressions.

This game requires some preparation by facilitators and pupils. The facilitator asks the pupils to find, in newspapers and magazines, pictures of faces with a range of emotions. They should bring their chosen picture to the circle. In order to have a range of pictures it may be necessary to dictate to individual pupils qualities to find such as someone looking stern, amused, frightened, bewildered etc.

Pupils then share their pictures and explain what it is in the facial expressions that indicate the emotion.

A sentence completion to follow this activity is:

'Something I have learnt about others' facial expressions is...'

Helpful hints

- It is possible to play this game with children in Key Stage I but it is best if in the first instance the pictures are provided.

- It is also important that the facial expressions in the pictures are unambiguous.

Finishing the Sentence

Aim: Encourages the development of awareness of one's own and others' emotional states, understanding others and building bonds, managing feelings, social skills and empathy.

The facilitator always starts and the sentence is taken up by each person in the circle. Choose from:

Self-awareness

My favourite food is...

My favourite animal is...

If I were an animal I would be... because...

If I were Prime Minister I'd...

The nicest thing anyone ever did for me was...

The best thing I ever did was...

I would love to...

If I were a magician I would...

I feel happy when...

I am bored when...

When I am older I would like to be...

If I wasn't here I would like to be...

If I were a car I'd be…

Sometimes I pretend that I am…

The best time I ever had was…

The best thing about school is…

The worst day ever had was…

My hero at the moment is… because…

If I was a piece of furniture I would be…

If I was a colour I would be…

A time I was really scared was when…

One person I'd like to spend the day with is…

It makes me angry when…

If I were a teacher I would…

The thing I enjoy doing most in school is…

The thing I enjoy doing most at home is…

It makes me feel good when…

I value people who…

All schools should teach…

One sport I would like to try is…

I would love to go on holiday to… because…

My favourite book is…

The thing that concerns me about school is…

Two words that best describe me are… and…

My favourite possession is… because…

Something I would like to achieve this year is…

One thing I would like people to remember me for is…

One thing I would like people to say about me is…

… is something I do well.

… is something I am getting better at.

The most important thing in my life is…

A goal I would like to have for myself is…

The best present I ever had was…

Three possessions I would like to take with me on a desert island would be…

When I am playing a game and I win I feel…

When I am playing a game and I lose I feel…

When I have to speak in front of everyone I feel…

When I share my crisps with someone I feel…

When I get my (Maths, English etc.) right I feel…

When I get my (Maths, English etc.) wrong I feel…

When I go into a new class I feel…

The kind of things I like to laugh at are…

I most dislike being told off when…

The most excited I have ever been was…

Awareness of others and empathy

The nicest thing I ever did for anyone is…

When my friend is sad I…

If I were a parent I would…

I think all children should…

One thing that would make this class better is if we…

One good thing about this class is…

One thing I would like this class to do is…

I like… because he/she…

I could be of help in the community by…

A good friend is someone who…

I was kind to… when I…

The best thing about my friend is…

I can be a friend by…

If my best friend was an animal he/she would be… because…

If my best friend was a piece of furniture it would be a... because...

I think a bully feels...

I think someone who is bullied feels...

If I know bullying is happening I feel...

When I fall out with other people I think they may feel...

People who have no friends feel...

If I know someone in my class without a friend I could...

The kinds of things that make me and my friends laugh are...

I can help others in this class that I am not friends with by...

I could make life easier for others by...

Handling relationships

When I'm angry at home I...

The sorts of things my family and I have fun with are...

Loyalty at home means...

I get fed up when my parents ask me to...

I am pleased when my parents ask me to...

I have fun with my brothers and sisters doing...

I admire my brother/sister when...

I get cross with my friends when...

I wish my parents would...

I get cross with my brother/sister when...

If my brother/sister left home I would miss them because...

I rely on my mum and dad for...

I could improve my relationship with my brother/sister by...

The best thing about my family is...

I am happiest with my family when...

I am happiest with my friends when...

One thing I would like my parents to say about me is...

One thing I hope my friends would say about me is...

The thing I most admire about my mum/dad is…

Making new friends is… because…

A good friend is someone who…

An ideal friend is…

When my friends and I fall out I…

A real friend would never ask you to…

If friends talk about me behind my back I…

I feel left out when…

Helpful hints

- When an activity mentions terms like 'parents', 'mother' or 'father' it is helpful to teach the group to substitute the name or term used to identify an alternative carer if appropriate.

- If the child is not ready to complete the sentence they can say 'pass' and you can return to them when you have finished the round. Encourage all children to take part.

- Choose statements that are suitable for the age and needs of the class.

Wishing Well

Aim: Encourages the development of emotional awareness of self and others, communication and listening.

You have just freed a genie from a bottle and you have got three wishes, one for yourself, one for your family and one for the whole world.

'For me I wish…'

'For my family I wish…'

'For the world I wish…'

Helpful hints

- Most groups' wishes will initially be about winning the lottery or having lots of money. You should allow time to express those ideas but this game can be focused to encourage more altruistic ideas and wishes, so you could play the game with a rule saying, for example, no wishes about money or only wishes for others less well off.

- This game is more suitable for the top end of Key Stage 2 and for Key Stage 3.

Guess Who

Aim: Encourages the development of self-awareness, social skills communication and understanding others.

Game 1

The facilitator starts by saying three things about someone in the circle, for example, it's a boy, his name begins with 'C', and he is good at making things.

When the three things have been said, any child who guesses the identity of the child described can raise a hand. If the guess is correct this child can then take a turn to describe another child.

The facilitator invites the children in the circle (especially the quiet ones) to have a go.

The children may need to be reminded to try not to make it too obvious by staring at the person they are describing.

Game 2

Before the session, the children and the facilitator write out some biographical information that describes them but does not make it too obvious who they are, i.e. include a description of the sort of person they think they are, their hobbies or unusual things about their family. (Put their name on the top corner.) When each person has done this, the pieces of paper are put into an envelope or box. Each Circle Time session the facilitator picks out three or four cards to read out for the class to guess.

Helpful hints

- This game is more suitable for Key Stage 2 and Key Stage 3. Be sure that the young people are used to the aims and philosophy of Circle Time and they understand the 'no put downs' rule.

- It is essential that children put their names on the paper. Some children will forget what they have written especially if it is three to four months before their information is read out, also their lives may have moved on. Check if the information is old that it is still relevant.

Enjoying and Achieving Games

These games help develop listening skills, cooperation, concentration and imagination. They are also fun.

50 Ways of Moving

Aim: Encourages the development of social skills, memory, taking turns, creative kinaesthetic thinking and bonds within the class.

Game 1

The facilitator sits in a circle with one extra chair or stands leaving a chair vacant.

The facilitator calls one person to start moving from his chair to the empty chair in any way he chooses, for example, hopping, jumping, or like an animal.

Another child across the circle from the empty chair is then chosen to move, trying not to copy the other person.

All children, including the facilitator, have a turn at moving in different ways to the empty chair.

Game 2

Two children at a time could be chosen to move to empty chairs.

It may be helpful to establish a rule, for example, no running.

Helpful hint

- For younger children this is a good game to follow on from Finishing the Sentence, for example, My favourite animal… You can then suggest they move like their animal.

Follow the Leader

Aim: Encourages the development of concentration, cooperation, following sequences, listening and ways of having fun.

The facilitator starts by saying, 'Watch me and do as I do'. Then he puts his hands on his lap, hands in the air, crosses a leg, and so on, giving children an idea of the sort of moves to make. The children copy. It may be necessary to suggest that they make their observations with a quick glance and avoid staring at the leader.

The facilitator explains the game. One person is chosen to go out of the room. Then one person is chosen to initiate the actions, e.g. hands on head, clapping, etc. Everyone copies the actions as though in unison so it is hard to guess the leader. This may take some practice.

The first person returns, stands in the centre of the circle and has three guesses at who is leading the actions. The facilitator then chooses two more people, one to go out and one to lead.

Helpful hints

- Some children love to be given the opportunity to lead others but it is a good way to give a shy child, or one having a bad time, a boost.

- This works better if the leader changes actions every 15 seconds.

Sleepmaker Detective

Aim: Encourages the development of cooperation, having fun and enjoyment, and calming down.

As with Follow the Leader, one person is chosen as a detective to wait outside the room. Then one person within the circle is chosen as 'The Sleepmaker'. When the detective outside the room returns, the Sleepmaker makes other children 'go to sleep' by winking at them. Circle participants indicate they have 'been put to sleep' by closing their eyes. The detective has to guess who the Sleepmaker is.

Helpful hints

- To move the game along a rule such as only three guesses might need to be introduced.

- An important rule is that when the Sleepmaker winks at you, you must cooperate by closing your eyes or at least looking down.

- Another rule may need to be that the effect of the Sleepmaker is to send you to sleep silently i.e. no snoring is needed.

Guarding the Keys

Aim: Encourages the development of listening skills, concentration and having fun together.

The facilitator explains that this game is all about being good listeners.

They are going to be listening for a positive sound of key jangling (demonstrate by jangling keys), not the sounds of footsteps or anyone moving.

The facilitator makes up a story about the keys, how important they are, what they are for, etc.

The children are asked to help guard these keys because someone in the circle is going to try and take them away.

The facilitator explains the game:

A bunch of keys is placed in the centre of the circle.

The children close their eyes, with no peeping. The facilitator keeps his/her eyes open to check no one peeps.

The facilitator taps a child on the shoulder, they open their eyes. That child then tries to pick up the keys without being heard.

When they can hear the sound of the keys being moved, without opening their eyes, children in the circle point to where the sound is coming from.

If pointed at directly, the child in the middle stops where she/he is.

The children all open their eyes. Those pointing to the noise are 'accurate listeners'.

The child replaces the keys in the middle and returns to his/her seat.

The facilitator then chooses another child to pick up the keys.

Helpful hint

- Set the scene for younger children by saying why your keys are important to you and why they need to be looked after.

Expressions

Aim: Encourages the development of perception of non-verbal body language and visual memory.

Game 1

The facilitator is the first person to make a face to the person on his left; this expression is copied. That person then turns to the person on his left and makes a face of his own.

The game is continued until all in the circle have copied a face and made one of their own.

Game 2

A variation of this can be to guess the emotion: that is the facilitator makes a face, the emotion has to be guessed. The child then makes a face indicating a different emotion and the next child in the circle has to guess the emotion.

The objective is to help children recognise how their feelings are reflected in their facial expression, and that a happy face not only makes them feel better but will also influence other people.

This can be extended by speculation on what might have caused the emotion, however this can be lengthy.

Helpful hint

- Children need to have an understanding of the feelings word you will be using, therefore before the game begins prepare them with a discussion about what the vocabulary means.

Listen and Touch

Aim: Encourages the development of listening, following directions and cooperating.

This game is for younger children.

The facilitator calls:

'Everyone touch… (a colour, person, object) with… (your thumb, little finger, elbow).'

Helpful hints

- It is important that the facilitator role models at first so that children can copy. Once they are all familiar with this game you can then just give the instruction.

- Concepts such as left and right can be introduced into this game.

Thunder

Aim: Encourages the development of following a sequence, listening and cooperating.

The facilitator leads the thunderstorm.

Each child must follow the person on their left. (Ensure the child knows who is to their left.)

The facilitator starts by rubbing their hands together saying, 'This is the sound of leaves rustling in the wind'. The person on his/her right then copies and it is repeated around the circle.

The facilitator then changes to tapping two fingers saying, 'Gentle rain begins to fall'.

Next the facilitator changes to clapping saying, 'The rain is getting harder and louder,' as clapping goes round the circle.

The hand clapping changes to thigh slapping, then stamping feet until all are doing the same action and saying, 'Rain is pouring, thunder is rolling.'

The circle then reverses the actions: feet stop, thigh slapping goes to hand clapping, to two finger tapping, to rustling leaves noise, then silence. Everyone puts their hands in their lap.

The storm has ceased.

Helpful hints

- Children in Key Stage 1 can play this game but they all have to follow the facilitator instead of one another.

- Facilitators can make a more elaborate story and invent new sounds.

The Wave

Aim: Encourages the development of cooperation, sequencing and having fun together.

This cooperative game is great fun and very impressive from the outside.

Everyone sits on the floor in a circle, leaning forward, with hands flat on the floor.

The facilitator's hands go up in the air then immediately back down to the floor. The next person copies the action of the facilitator, and so on in quick succession.

Helpful hint

- Choose about six pupils to demonstrate when you first play this game with your class.

Magic Box

Aim: Encourages the development of creativity, non-verbal communication and taking turns.

This is a mime game.

The facilitator places an imaginary box into the middle of the circle and lifts the lid.

She/he silently demonstrates an object taken from the box, for example, a baby, a football, a banana.

The children then raise their hands when they guess the object.

The child who guesses correctly takes something from the magic box and mimes it.

Helpful hints

- The facilitator needs to demonstrate this game first allowing them all to guess together.

- They need to be reminded again before the game starts that they must put up their hand when they have guessed without calling out.

Let's Laugh

Aim: Encourages the development of managing feelings and having fun together.

This game involves trying to get someone to laugh (without touching).

One person stands in the centre of the circle with the intention of not laughing.

The people in the circle take turns to ask the person in the middle questions, for example, 'What do you brush your teeth with?'

The person in the centre always answers with, 'Sausages' or 'Pink frogs', or something else that is silly.

If the person in the centre laughs then she/he must change places with someone else, and so on.

Helpful hint

- Limit the number of tries at making someone laugh to three, otherwise the game can take too long for some players.

Don't Smile!

Aim: Encourages the development of managing feelings and having fun together.

Game 1

Children are divided into pairs and labelled A and B. It is the job of the person who is B to make A smile without using words. A tries not to smile.

Game 2

Someone is designated as 'it' and it is their job to make people in the circle smile with out using words. The first person to smile becomes 'it'.

Helpful hint

- Game 2 should be a fast moving game with lots of classmates having a turn. Include the rule that you only have one go. If someone who has had a go is the first to smile then they nominate someone else who has not yet had a go.

Finishing Games

These games provide an opportunity to end the session in a cooperative way.

Finishing Games

Aim: Encourages the development of cooperation and building bonds.

Game 1: Pass the Smile

The facilitator turns to the person on their right, makes eye contact and smiles, that person turns to person on their right and smiles, until everyone in the circle has had a turn.

Game 2: Pass the Squeeze

The facilitator decides whether it will begin from the their left or right side.

Everyone in the circle joins hands.

The facilitator starts by gently squeezing the hand of the person next to them, then the squeeze is passed around the circle as quickly as possible without a sound (like an electric current).

Game 3: Blind Squeeze

Once children are familiar with passing the squeeze then they can do it with their eyes shut. This takes a good deal of trust. This is a very good activity to help develop a sense of togetherness and group cohesion within the class.

Helpful hint

- In Pass the Squeeze keep joined hands in view so that the squeeze can be watched as it goes around.

Part 2

The Development of Circle Time

Circle Time will give class groups practice at being assertive instead of aggressive and experience of feelings of respect and acceptance from one another. It will help them have a more receptive and caring attitude to each other. It will also encourage increased personal responsibility for behaviour.

It is at this point that the teacher will be able to move the class into becoming a group that is ready to be more autonomous and make decisions for themselves. Problems and concerns can be brought to the group for discussion and resolution.

If Circle Time is used regularly and children are encouraged by the teacher to work non-judgementally and to listen with respect to one another, considerable trust as well as cooperation within the class group will develop over a period of time. The children's articulation of feelings and needs will have helped awareness of themselves and their peers.

Themes

Below are some ideas for developing the work that takes place during Circle Time. There may be particular problems or issues that need to be dealt with for the class. We give examples of how the games can be used to deal with some very serious issues. It needs to be explained that a theme will be taken for the session. It is best that the teacher should be the facilitator in the first instance.

Developing a Sense of 'Us': Relationships in Class

The friendships that children make at school can be very significant to them. Indeed they can last a lifetime. The teaching and curriculum content can be of the highest quality but if children are worried or anxious about broken friendships amongst their peers their ability to optimalise their learning will be impaired. As most teachers know, a great deal of valuable learning time can be wasted when children are upset by classroom relationships.

This theme explores ideas about classroom relationships.

Note: Before you use Circle Time to deal with an issue such as this, it will be important for the children to be aware of the Circle Time process and what is expected of them. Do not select potentially upsetting issues in Circle Time unless you and the class are used to using it and understand the process.

Ground rules

Remind everyone of the rules of Circle Time. For example:

- We listen when someone else is speaking.

- There are no put downs.

- We may pass.

Ensure everyone understands the rules. In our experience the 'No put downs' rule is not always understood by everyone even in Year 6.

Aims

- Creating an emotionally safe and supportive environment. This will be essential for work on friendships to be successful.

- Exploring the theme of friendships.

- Deciding collectively upon a way for all the pupils in the class to manage their relationships.

Warm up: Silent Statements

We often introduce a theme through this core game. It starts us off in a non-threatening way and sends out the message that no one will be named or in any way shamed.

The facilitator begins by saying:

'Change places all those who…'

'…consider friends to be important to them.'

'…think they are a good friend.'

Finishing the Sentence

This is another core game. It can be used to raise issues about the way children relate to one another, develop some awareness of how they perform as friends and what makes a good friend.

Statement 1   A friend is someone who…

Statement 2   I hope my friends will…

Statement 3   I am a good friend when…

Statement 4   Something I like to do with my friends in the playground is..

Statement 5   In this class if I need help it is good to have a friend who…

Statement 6   Good friends make school better because…

Statement 7   Teachers can help us to be friends by…

Partners

This is a core game that can be adapted to the theme. Divide the class into pairs. If there are an equal number of children then the facilitator watches, if not then the facilitator partners one of the children.

The children can discuss a range of friendship issues. Examples of what they could be asked to do are:

Game 1

Identify two attributes that you both agree make someone a good friend and be ready to report to the rest of the class.

Children will report by using a sentence stub such as:

'We think a good friend...'

Game 2

Identify two attributes that you both agree make someone a poor friend and be ready to report to the rest of the class.

Children will report by using a sentence stub such as:

'We think a poor friend...'

Game 3

Identify two things that you both agree you do not like having to do and be ready to report to the rest of the class.

Children will report by using a sentence stub such as:

'We don't like having to...'

When the partners have reported back to the circle the facilitator can then open up the discussion to enable the children to explore their thoughts and feelings about friendship and how they make friends. They can be encouraged to think about kindness, and treating others how they would like to be treated, to develop a sense of belonging and 'a sense of us'.

Managing Feelings and Developing Relationships

Successful schools create an ethos where it is possible for pupils to feel safe, feel they belong and have areas of school life where they can achieve and succeed. Circle Time can meet these needs particularly when it is part of a developmental curriculum. Emotionally literate children are better equipped as teenagers and adults to sustain relationships and go on to build their own emotionally literate families. Neuroscience has helped us understand how much, on entering school, there is of a young child's brain to still develop. Schooling can make a positive contribution to social conditioning. It can have an impact on attitudes and beliefs and it can help to develop resilience.

Developing a positive self-esteem has long been recognised as desirable. Recalling Maslow's (1987) hierarchy of needs, children's needs are for security, self-identity, belonging to a group, acceptance within one's community, achieving a sense of purpose in life and having identified areas of competence. Applying the skills of emotional intelligence such as self-awareness, managing our feelings, social skills and empathy are important to most aspects of developing a positive self-esteem and achieving within Maslow's hierarchy.

The sample session below gives ideas for developing children's thinking on managing their own feelings, reading others' feelings and how to sustain friendships.

Managing feelings

The first step to managing feelings is to identify and label feelings. It is necessary to develop an affective vocabulary to be able to label the feelings that have been identified.

Use the following introductory games:

My Friend is Feeling

Pair the children A and B. Ask the children to discuss with each other how they are feeling. Tell them they must listen well because they will be asked to remember what has been said so that they can tell all those sitting in the circle how their partner is feeling.

Child A introduces child B saying:

> 'This is... today she/he is feeling...'

Sentence Completions

'I can tell… (friend's name) is happy when…'

'I show I am happy when…'

'I can tell… (friend's name) is sad when…'

How are they Feeling?

This game requires some preparation by the teachers and pupils. Ask the pupils to find in newspapers and magazines pictures of faces with a range of emotions. They should bring their chosen picture to the circle. In order to have a range of pictures it may be necessary to dictate to individual pupils qualities to find such as someone looking stern, amused, frightened or bewildered.

Pupils then share their pictures and explain what it is in the facial expressions that indicate the emotion.

Use this sentence completion to follow this activity:

'Something I have learnt about facial expressions is…'

New Feeling Words

Again this requires some preparation. Pupils find for themselves a word they did not know before that describes a feeling. The new word is brought to the circle. Children are divided into pairs. They mime their feeling word and their partner tries to guess the new word.

Children need to be reassured that they may not guess the exact word.

Conclude this activity with the following sentence completions:

'My word was easy/difficult to mime because…'

'My word was… and it means…'

'I have/have never felt like this before.'

How I Manage Feelings

'When my brother/sister upsets me I manage this well when I…'

'When my brother/sister upsets me I manage this badly by…'

Developing a Vocabulary for Emotions

Baron-Cohen and colleagues at Cambridge University have found 1512 emotion words in the English language. From this they have identified 412 as distinct emotional concepts which can be placed into 24 emotional groups (in Maines 2003). The groups are:

afraid	happy	sorry
angry	hurt	sure
bored	interested	surprised
bothered	kind	thinking
disbelieving (sceptical)	liked	touched
disgusted	romantic	unfriendly
excited	sad	unsure
fond	sneaky	wanting

It is suggested that a helpful way of thinking about these words is to imagine them as being a part of the colour spectrum which is comprised of groups of colours such as the red group, the yellow group and so on. Within each group there are shades of colours such as turquoise and aquamarine in the blue group. Thus every emotion falls into a specific group, e.g. grumpy and furious are in the angry group.

Group	Emotion words Key Stage 1 (5 to 7 year olds)							
afraid		afraid	worried					
angry		grumpy	moaning	moody				teasing
bored								
disgusted								
excited								
fond		liking						
happy		comfortable	glad	joking	lucky	merry	safe	
hurt		bullied	hated					
interested		asking	believing	listening				
kind		friendly	helpful	polite				
liked								
sad	lonely	lost	sad	tired	upset			
sneaky								
sorry								
sure	honest	strong	sure					
surprised								
thinking								
unfriendly	bullying	difficult	hateful	mean	unfriendly	unkind		
unsure	shy	silly	unsure					
wanting	greedy	wanting						

Group	Emotion Words Key Stage 2 (7 to 11 year olds)						
afraid	desperate	nervous	threatened				
angry	annoyed	complaining	furious	wild			
excited	adventurous	lively					
fond	loving	trusting					
happy	calm playful	cheeky pleasure	cheered proud	delighted	enjoying	fine	grateful
hurt	attacked	blamed	cheated	ignored	relaxed		
interested	concentrating						
kind	caring	giving					
liked	forgiven	welcomed					
sad	disappointed	tearful					
sneaky	lying						
sorry	ashamed	embarrassed	guilty				
sure	bossy	decided	serious				
surprised	shocked						
thinking	dreamy	thoughtful					
unfriendly	blaming threatening	cold violent	cruel	disliking	ignoring	scolding	selfish
unsure	confused	puzzled	uncomfortable				
wanting	begging	hopeful	jealous				

65

Group	Emotion Words Key Stage 3 (11 to 14 year olds)						
afraid	cowardly	dreading	frantic	jumpy	panicked	terrified	watchful
angry	displeased	explosive	frustrated				
bored	unimpressed	distant					
bothered	bothered	impatient					
disbelieving	disbelieving	doubtful	questioning	suspicious			
excited	enthusiastic	keen					
fond	affectionate	close	respectful				
happy	amused	content	easy-going	mischievous	positive	relieved	
hurt	betrayed	broken	criticised	disbelieved	dislike	disrespectful	
interested	absorbed	curious	fascinated	impressed	tempted		
kind	calming understanding	cheering warm	comforting welcoming	concerned willing	encouraging	forgiving	patient
liked	adored supported	appreciated wanted	comforted	included	needed	praised	rewarded
romantic	attracted	bewitched	romantic				
sad	discouraged heartbroken	hysterical withdrawn	gloomy	troubled	heartache	weak	homesick
sneaky	humouring	mysterious	tempting				
sorry	responsible						
sure	competitive	persuaded	prepared	pushy	stubborn		
surprised	dazed	horrified	startled	wonder			
thinking	judging						
touched	soppy	touched					
unfriendly	aggressive uncaring	argumentative	detesting	disapproving	disrespectful	humiliating	rude
unsure	clueless	undecided					
wanting	demanding	wishful					

For information about the work of Simon Baron-Cohen and his research visit www.autismresearchcentres.com

Friendships

Introductory game: This is My Friend

Children introduce themselves and a friend sitting next to them:

'I am… and this is…'

Sentence Completions

Positive aspects:

Key Stage 1   'I like my friend because… '

Key Stage 2   'A good friend would always…'

Key Stage 3   'A quality I admire in a friend is…'

Negative aspects:

Key Stage 1   'I am sad if my friend…'

Key Stage 2   'I fall out with my friends when…'

Key Stage 3   'A good friend would never…'

Activity: things we have in common

Use one of the worksheets on the following pages to help children find others in the class who can agree to the statements. A different name is needed for each statement.

Children in Key Stage 1 write the names of classmates. Those in Key Stage 2 and Key Stage 3 get a signature.

These pages are samples. It is fun for the children to make up their own questions individually or in groups.

Once the sheets have been filled in gather everyone into a circle to explore the answers on their sheets.

Everyone in the circle should have the chance to respond to the following questions:

- Did anyone find it difficult to find someone for any of the questions?
- Did they find out anything new about anyone?
- Were there any surprises?

Web Masters: use one of these games.

Concluding game: Pass the Smile.

Key Stage 1

Finding Things in Common

Find someone who:

Has a tooth missing ....

Has blue eyes ....

Has long hair ....

Has the same size hand as you ....

Can count to 20 ....

Finding Things in Common

Collect the signature of someone who:

Has a pet ....

Has a brother/sister in another class in school ....

Is taller than you ....

Can play a musical instrument ....

Has the same colour eyes as you ....

Likes eating pizza ....

Likes watching cartoons ....

Can ride a bike ....

Finding Things in Common

Collect the signature of someone who:

Is as tall as you ....

Enjoys the same music as you ....

Likes using computers ....

Can skateboard ....

Likes eating chocolate ....

Can play a musical instrument ....

Does not like watching football ....

Walks to school..

Arguing and Fighting

This is an issue that arises frequently with young people. Mostly they sort out problems among themselves. However, very often after such problems have been sorted out there has been a winner and a loser. In such scenarios usually there are residual feelings of anger, resentment, guilt or disappointment. To deal with this you could start with Silent Statements and Finishing Sentences that focus on feelings.

Silent Statements

Change places if...

... you feel angry when you don't get your own way.

... you feel upset at being called names.

... you have seen two people fighting/arguing in this class.

Finishing Sentences

'I feel... when I fall out with a friend.'

'I feel... when I think a friend has been unkind.'

'I feel... when I see two members of the class arguing.'

'I feel... when I hear someone called names.'

'I feel... when I am called names.'

Using 'I' messages – label the act, not the person

Circle Time can be used to help children use 'I' messages; they fit in well with this theme. The use of 'I' messages can be used very effectively when we want to change someone's behaviour because there is a conflict. The 'You' messages that we often use can be confrontational and offer no solution and do not suggest a better way of behaving. They are usually an emotional response and are not very informational or effective. For children with low self-esteem they are another confirmation of the poor image they have of themselves.

'I' messages are effective for the following reasons:

- They are a good basis to encourage the will to change.

- The behaviour is disapproved of rather than the person.

- They are not confrontational.

- They help preserve the relationship.

- They encourage calm communication.

- They allow us to communicate our feelings.

An 'I' message has three components:

1. Behaviour

2. Effect

3. Feelings.

For example:

When you shout out... (behaviour)

it interrupts the lesson... (effect)

and I feel irritated... (feelings)

Sometimes it is helpful to add a solution, for example:

'When you shout out it interrupts the lesson and I feel irritated. I will answer your questions when I've finished.'

When we communicate in this way we are less likely to shout as we are sometimes tempted to do with a 'You' message, i.e. YOU sit down and be quiet.

'I' messages need to be practised but are such an effective way of communicating for teachers, parents and children.

In our experience young people find it easier to say how they feel first, then name the behaviour and its effect.

The children (and the teachers) can practise this in pairs during Circle Time. Give a situation to respond to, for example:

- How can we respond to someone calling us names?

Feeling	Behaviour	Effect
I feel really unhappy...	*when you call me names...*	*and I get left out.*

- How can we respond to someone pushing in?

Feeling	Behaviour	Effect
I feel really fed up...	*when you push in...*	*because it makes me knock into the person behind, they fall over and we all get into trouble.*

- How can we respond to someone who refuses to share?

Feeling	Behaviour	Effect
I feel mad...	*when you don't share and let me have a turn...*	*because it will end up with my finding someone else to play with.*

Stealing

This is a problem that crops up in all schools from time to time. You may or may not know who is responsible, but you can begin to deal with the feelings it generates within the group and how the thief and victim may feel. It is important to avoid inadvertent name-calling or labelling, for example, a sentence completion beginning: 'a thief is...' or 'a victim is...' is labelling and should not be used.

It is as damaging to label the victim as it is to label the thief. It is always more productive to work on feelings.

It is safer to start working without words, so use Silent Statements such as:

Change places...

 ... if you are aware stealing has happened

 ... if stealing worries you

 ... if stealing does not worry you

 ... if you or a friend have had anything stolen.

Never ask for public confessions.

Next you can move on to Finishing Sentences, for example:

 'I think a thief may feel...'

 'I think it would feel... to have something stolen'.

 'I feel... knowing stealing is happening.'

Bullying

Bullying needs extreme caution and care in handling. There is an excellent video and accompanying workbook by Maines and Robinson (1992) suggested in the reference section. Taylor (2003) found that, 'Listening in the circle to another child's expression of feelings about being bullied made them think again about their behaviour' (p 149).

It will depend upon your reasons for raising this theme how you choose to follow the games. It may be an awareness raising exercise or you may have become aware that there is bullying happening in a particular class.

Note: Before you use Circle Time to deal with an issue such as bullying that has taken place in your class, it will be important for the children to be aware of the Circle Time process and what is expected of them. Do not pick up on such an emotive and potentially upsetting issue in Circle Time unless you and the class are used to using it.

Ground rules

Remind everyone of the rules of Circle Time. For example:

- We listen when someone else is speaking.
- There are no put downs.
- We may pass.

Ensure everyone understands the rules. In our experience the 'No put downs' rule is not always understood by everyone even in Year 6.

Aims

- Creating an emotionally safe and supportive environment. This will be essential for work on bullying to be successful.
- Exploring the theme of bullying.
- Deciding collectively upon a way forward.

Warm up

Start the session with a fun game such as Silent Statements or another of the mixing up games.

Activity: what is bullying?

This activity will generate a common understanding for all and will provide you with a basis on which to work. Before you introduce this section you may want to establish a new rule.

- No one is to be identified by name.

Begin by saying you want to explore the theme of bullying with the class. You will expect this to take one or two or however many sessions you decide. It will be worth emphasising:

- This is not about an individual.

- You do not want names of anyone in this class or any other class.

This is not a name and shame activity. If pupils want to talk to you in private after Circle Time then they may.

A sentence completion about bullying will help to be clear about how this group of children perceive bullying. A sentence stub such as: 'I think bullying is…' will generate a list of unpleasant activities. You may want to record them on a flip-chart but it is not essential.

It may be helpful to have a short discussion about agreeing some shared definitions such as 'bullying is something that happens over a period of time, it is not a one-off incident'. Then you may agree a list of activities such as:

- being left out

- called names

- hit

- having equipment taken.

Silent Statements

It is possible to use Silent Statements to introduce this theme. It is a powerful, safe way to introduce the theme. It will enable the group to share knowledge without words. Examples of statements might be, stand up and change places all those:

- who know bullying has taken place in this school

- who know bullying has taken place in this class

- who have themselves seen bullying happening.

These statements gradually draw the theme closer from the school in general to an individual eyewitness. You may want to stop there and continue with the theme at your next session. Sometimes it is more useful to go gently and allow thinking time in between sessions.

Other Silent Statements may include, stand up and change places if these statements apply to you:

- I am sometimes worried about bullying.

- I have seen people being bullied.

- Bullying happens in our playground.

- Bullying happens in our class.

- Being deliberately left out is bullying.

- Bullying is a problem in our school.

- Teachers can make things worse if you tell them about bullying.

Statement Line

This is different form of Silent Statements and it allows another way for the teacher to explore the theme without words.

Indicate an imaginary line across the circle. Mark one end as 'strongly agree' and the other end as 'strongly disagree'. The children stand on the 'line' depending on how they agree with your statement. You can adapt the Silent Statements, for example:

- I know bullying takes place in this school.

- I know bullying has taken place in this class.

- I think name-calling can be worse than physically bullying.

- Teachers make things worse if you tell them.

Never ask for details about the statements made but you can follow this with a general discussion about distribution on the Statement Line.

Feelings

Bullying generates very strong feelings in all those it touches. The next two games do not encourage pupils to identify any individual but they do allow pupils to explore feelings.

Game 1

Divide the class into pairs. Ask them to decide how a bully and someone who has been bullied might feel then to feed back with a sentence stub:

'A bully might feel…'

'Someone who is bullied might feel…'

Game 2

In this work, the role of onlooker is often missed. A sentence completion activity about the role of onlooker will explore this role:

'Onlookers might feel…'

A general discussion about these roles might help clarify things for individual pupils. Some points might include:

- We are all victims of bullying when it happens, including onlookers.

- Individual people, because of personalities, outlook on life and so on, react differently to similar situations.

- Some cope better than others.

What can we do about bullying?

These activities are intended to move the group on. Briefly talk to the group about the fact that:

- Bullying can often happen in children's groups and adult's groups.

- Everyone can be responsible for preventing it.

- Group disapproval and a cultural change is one of the most powerful ways of stopping it when everyone treats everyone else with respect.

Explore options through a sentence completion. Divide the class into threes and ask the groups to discuss what the following people could do to stop bullying:

The onlooker	'Onlookers could...'
The bully	'Bullies could...'
The person being bullied	'Person being bullied could...'

You may need a discussion about the question, does the bully want to do anything to stop or change? Very often bullies are pleased when adults intervene and stop what is happening.

Write the ideas on a flip-chart. Continuing with groups of three, choose things that the pupils think could be:

- done immediately by themselves

- followed up by teachers

- followed up by the class.

From these discussions you can generate a class charter of rights and responsibilities.

Statement Line

Use an imaginary line drawn through the centre of a circle. At one end is 'strongly disagree' at the other is 'strongly agree'.

- Bullying has reduced in this class.

- Bullying continues to happen among some people.

- If we work together we could continue to improve things.

Other Themes

Before you take a theme with the class make a careful plan setting out the sentences you will use to develop the theme and the non-verbal responses you will ask of the group.

There are many themes you can explore, for example:

- new experiences

- rules at home

- changing schools

- anger

- sibling rivalry

- relationships with teachers

- homework

- rules at school

- bullying.

Suggestion box

You can provide a box for the young people to add their own ideas and themes.

Small Group Work in Circle Time for Dealing with Difficult Situations

Dealing with 'difficult situations' enables young people to put themselves in someone else's shoes, learn about coping with conflict and communicate effectively with their peer groups and others. It develops their competence to become self-aware, manage their feelings and become motivated. It develops their social competence so that they can learn how to handle relationships and appreciate the needs and feeling of others.

It may be helpful to have details of outside agencies and be able to describe their role if the opportunity arises. Any suitable literature about these agencies should be available to everyone. Be aware that this may prompt individual approaches for this information.

Divide the circle into groups of three or four. Go around the circle giving each child a number from one to three, or four. Ask all those given the number one to move with their chairs to one part of the room, all those given the number two to another part of the room and so on.

Give each group a short scenario of a 'difficult situation' and ask them to decide how they would deal with it. A pen and paper may be useful here to write their solutions so that they remember when their turn comes. Ask them to nominate one person in the group to read out the situation to the circle at the end and another person to give their solution.

Allow about ten minutes before they rejoin the circle.

Difficult situation scenarios

1. You are really fed up because you have been given a detention in class for something you have not done. You know it was the person sitting behind you.

What would you do?

2. Your mum is always telling you that you are not as clever as your brother. You know your reading isn't that good but you feel really hurt because you are working as hard as you can.

What would you do?

3. My best friend has started to go off with another group at lunchtime leaving me on my own. When I try at tag along they ignore me and I feel left out and upset.

What would you do?

4. Your friend has seemed very unhappy recently. She has been much quieter than usual and does not join in with the group when you are having fun together. She avoids you at lunchtimes and goes off on her own. Yesterday you saw her throwing her sandwiches in the bin. She looks pale and thin. You have tried asking her what is the matter but she won't say.

What would you do?

5. I went to town with some of my friends on Saturday and we went into a shop for some sweets and a drink. When we came out they had all taken

something extra without paying for it. They wanted me to go back in and take something as well but I didn't go and they laughed and teased me. I felt left out and uncomfortable for the rest of the afternoon.

What would you do?

6. The new girl in our class is a bit weird. She doesn't like talking about clothes, make-up, music or boys and walks away when we try to include her in our conversation. She never says anything about herself and now one of the girls in our group has started calling her names and whispering loudly to others about her so that she can hear. Yesterday at breaktime I saw her in the toilet crying. I felt embarrassed about what had happened but I don't want to tell the others this in case they pick on me.

What can I do?

7. Mum is always picking on me for one thing or another; whatever I do is wrong. Whenever my younger brother and I have a row he always goes off crying to her and I get the blame; it's not fair. I feel like running away.

What can I do?

8. I come into school on the bus. There is a girl on the bus, I don't know her name, she is in the year above me and she is really horrible to me. She calls me names, takes my bag and throws it down the aisle, pushes me when I get on or off the bus and I'm really scared of her. The others just laugh and think it's a big joke. I can't tell anyone because she lives near me and I see her when I go to the shop and she calls me names then as well. No one can stop her. I just don't want to come to school anymore.

What can I do?

When the time is up the groups rejoin the circle. Ask each group in turn to read out their situations and how they would deal with it. Open up the discussion to all the groups to share ideas before moving on to the next one.

Helpful hint

- Using 'I' messages would be useful in this exercise.

References

Ballard, J. (1982). *Circle Book: A Leader Hand Book for Conducting Circle Time. A Curriculum of Effect.* New York, NY: Rivington.

Bliss, T., Robinson, G. and Maines, B. (1995) *Developing Circle Time.* Bristol. Lucky Duck Publishing.

Booth-Church, E., (2003). *Best-Ever Circle Time Activities: Back To School.* New York. Scholastic.

Burns, D. (1982). *Self Concept Development and Education.* Sydney. Holt, Rinehart and Winston.

Button, K., Winter, M., (2004) *Pushing Back the Furniture.* Bristol. Lucky Duck Publishing.

Bromfield, C., Curry, M. (1994) *Personal and Social Education for Primary Schools Through Circle Time.* NASEN.

Canfield, J. and Wells, H. (1976). *100 Ways to Enhance Self Concept in the Classroom.* New Jersey. Prentice-Hall.

C.A.S.E. (1999). *Six Years of Circle Time.* Bristol. Lucky Duck Publishing.

Burt, S., *Six More Years of Circle Time.* Bristol. Lucky Duck Publishing.

Cooperation in the Classroom – a project pack for teachers. Global Cooperation for a Better World. 98, Tennyson Road, London NW6 7SB.

Cremin, H. (2002). Circle Time: why it doesn't always work. *Primary Practice,* 30, 23-8

DFES/1089/2005 G. *Excellence and Enjoyment: Social and Emotional Aspects of Learning.*

DFES/1379/2004. *Every Child Matters: Change for Children In Schools*

Games, Games, Games. Produced by The Woodcraft Folk.

Goleman, D. (1995) *Emotional Intelligence. Why it Can Matter More than I.Q.* London, Bloomsbury.

Lawrence, D. (1973). *Improved Reading through Counselling Work.* London, Ward Lock.

Lawrence, D. (1988). *Enhancing Self-esteem in the Classroom.* London, Paul Chapman Publishing.

Masheder, M. (1986). *Let's Cooperate.* Peace Education.

Masheder, M. (1989). *Let's Play Together.* London, Green Print, The Merlin Press Ltd.

Maines, B. (2003). *Reading Faces and Learning about Human Emotions.* Bristol, Lucky Duck Publishing.

Maines, B. and Robinson, G. (1992). *Michael's Being Bullied, The No Blame Approach.* Bristol, Lucky Duck Publishing.

Mosley, J. (1996) *Quality Circle Time.* Wisbech, LDA.

Qualifications and Curriculum Authority (2002). *Personal, Social and Health Education and Citizenship at Key stages 1 and 2: Initial Guidance for Schools.* London, QCA

Qualifications and Curriculum Authority (2002). *Citizenship: a Scheme of work for Key stages 1 and 2.* London, QCA.

Purkey, W. (1970). *Self Concept and School Achievement.* New Jersey, Prentice-Hall.

Robinson, G. and Maines, B., (1988). *A Bag of Tricks,* the video and handbook. Bristol, Lucky Duck Publishing.

Robinson, G. and Maines, B., (1999). *Circle Time Resources.* Bristol, Lucky Duck Publishing.

Smith, C., (2003) *Introducing Circle Time to Secondary Students: A Seven Lesson programme for 11 to 12 Year Olds.* Bristol, Lucky Duck Publishing Ltd.

Smith, C., (2003) *Concluding Circle Time with Secondary Students: A Seven Lesson programme for 13 to 14 Year Olds.* Bristol, Lucky Duck Publishing.

Smith, C., (2003) *More Circle Time for Secondary Students: A Seven Lesson programme for 12 to 13 Year Olds.* Bristol, Lucky Duck Publishing.

Taylor, M. (2003) *Going Round in Circles.* Slough. NFER.

Ways and means; an approach to problem solving. The Handbook of Kingston Friends Workshop Group.

Weatherhead, Y., (2004) *Enriching Circle Time.* Bristol, Lucky Duck Publishing.

White, M. (1999) *Magic Circles.* Bristol, Lucky Duck Publishing.

More Circle Time Books from Lucky Duck

Music in the Circle

Using Music, Rhythm, Rhyme and Song in Circle Time

Margaret Collins

These activities use Circle Time techniques to help children use and learn about rhythm, songs, instruments, story projects and much more.
April 2006 • 75 pages
Paper (1-4129-1908-8)

Circle Time for the Very Young

For Nursery, Reception and Key Stage 1 Children

Margaret Collins

'It has very clear activities and progressions with activities to encourage children to share ideas in solving real life situations. It is very user friendly' - **SNIP**
2001 • 101 pages
Paper (1-87394-253-2)

Enhancing Circle Time for the Very Young

For Nursery, Reception and Key Stage 1 Children

Margaret Collins

Encourages children to focus on the content of Circle Time as a way of sharing their work, ideas and thoughts.
2003 • 108 pages
Paper (1-904315-17-8)

Six Years of Circle Time

A Developmental Primary Curriculum - Produced by a Group of Teachers in Cardiff

Graham Davies

Provides a structured, step-by-step curriculum framework, with games and activities at every stage.
1999 • 112 pages
Paper (1-87394-252-4)

Circle Time Resources

Book and CD

George Robinson and **Barbara Maines**

This copiable resource contains three different sets of materials that can be reproduced onto paper for a one-off activity, or copied onto card for frequent use.
1998 • 94 pages
Paper (1-87394-237-0)

Success into Secondary

Supporting Transition with Circle Time

Cherrie Demain and **Lorraine Hurst**

The 6 sessions with follow-up activities are based on a Circle Time approach to help children make the transition from primary education.
2004 • 54 pages
Paper (1-904315-28-3)

Circle Time for Adolescents

A Seven Session Programme for 14 to 16 Year Olds

Charlie Smith

The fourth book in Charlie Smith's Circle Time for Secondary Schools series addresses the transition from Key Stage 3 to Key Stage 4.
2004 • 114 pages
Paper (1-904315-27-5)

Just the Same on the Inside

Understanding Diversity and Supporting Inclusion in Circle Time

Margaret Collins and Juan Bornman

Includes a series of stories about children with disabilities accompanied by explanations of the nature and causes of their difficulties.
2004 • 110 pages
Paper (1-904315-56-9)

Circling Round Citizenship

PSHE Activities for 4-8 Year-Olds to use in Circle Time

Margaret Collins

Using the Circle Time framework Margaret Collins has developed active ways to deliver elements of the PSHE and citizenship curriculum.
2002 • 102 pages
Paper (1-87394-259-1)

Coming Round to Circle Time

...The Video Makes it Come Alive!

Video and Booklet

Teresa Bliss, George Robinson and **Barbara Maines**

This video material adds feel and flavour to Circle Time through watching question and answer sessions.
1995 • 10 pages
Cloth (1-87394-238-9)

Please visit our website at www.paulchapmanpublishing.co.uk for more Circle Time resources!